Disagree and Stay in Love

Liz SuperLibrarian

Livre

'The best gift you can give your family is a happy relationship.'

Liz SuperLibrarian

Learn to

fight fair

and

your relationship

will

last forever.

Problems can sometimes feel overwhelming.

It's ok to have

disagreements

and

arguments.

Take a close look at yourself,
and ask - do I fight fair?

Use easy tips to fight fair
and stay together.

Take arguments to a private place...

and keep arguments private.

No put-downs or name calling.

Start your sentence with...

'I feel...'

No destructive criticism

or physical abuse!

WALK AWAY to calm down.

Put it in writing,

write a letter, email or text.

Avoid yelling in front of your kids...

because it can scare and upset them.

If you are going to lose your temper... WALK AWAY!

... and count to 100.

Return when you are
calm and ready to talk.

Instead of complaining about what you don't want...

ask for what you do want.

Life isn't black and white,

check your thinking...

find a middle ground.

all or
nothing

‘Am I

stuck in

negative

thinking?’

I can change my thinking.

Tackle the problem...

...not the person.

Deal with problems
while they are small,
before they get **bigger**.

Stay on the problem
at hand.

Don't get off track
with other issues.

中央区
伏見町

Don't allow an argument to become a blasting match about past events.

Stay in the present

and keep it relevant.

Keep the volume down.

Give arguments a time limit.

End arguments
in a good spirit.

Stop arguments in
front of family members.

Give them a
face-saving
way out...
make a joke.

Stop talking if the words get out of control, take a break.

Can't agree?

...talk to someone who can help.

A counsellor, priest, trusted friend or family member.

Feeling upset or
stuck in a problem

Ask yourself...

‘How can I see the problem differently?’

‘What can I learn from the problem?’

Can’t face the problem?

Ask yourself…

‘What is good about the problem?’

Not coping?

Don't wait
for the fall...
ask for help.

We all need help sometimes.

Don't play the
blame game,
it's a loser's game.

Don't bad mouth your partner behind their back.

Instead, ask yourself...

'What can I do to make things better?'

If you win and

your partner loses...

your relationship loses.

This means you lose!

Don't say
you can't
control
your temper...

it's that you don't control your temper.

The only person you <u>can</u> control is you.

Don't be pig-headed,

admit when you are wrong.

Apologise as soon as possible when you are wrong.

Avoid being
a right fighter.

Do you want
to be right
and alone?

Stop and think...

let small things go,

most arguments are

about small stuff.

Forgiveness is a choice,
not a feeling.

Choose to forgive,
every relationship
needs a hero.

Let it go and move on.

Feel free from the past.

Relationships require work...

the first person you need

to work on is you!

Your partner will see
your effort and be more
likely to make an effort.

Smile first.

Don't wait for somone else
to make you smile.

See the big picture...
your time will end one day.

Don't become another

divorcc statistic.

Be the ones that made it.

Always end arguments
on good terms.

Don't be stubborn.

Be the one to kiss and make up first.

We all make mistakes.

Kiss everyday!

Try to see the
other's point of view.

First try to understand...

walk in their shoes.

Then ask to be understood...

... so they can walk in your shoes.

Life can sometimes be unfair.

But you can be fair to yourself...

Embrace one tip a week.

When you know better...

...life is better.

Think of 3 things you
love about your partner.

When you give LOVE,
LOVE comes back to you.

First Published in 2014 by Livre Publishing

Liz SuperLibrarian

Disagree and Stay in Love

ISBN 978-0-977-5872-78

Designed by Simon Creedy

Livre Publishing

PO Box A240 Sydney South NSW 1235

www.livre.com.au

Printed by Bright Print Group

PRINTED IN AUSTRALIA